Faithful Innovation
Leader Companion

Copyright © 2022 by Faith+Lead of Luther Seminary

Luther Seminary retains the ownership and copyright of the contents of this book. These materials may be reproduced and distributed in print or digital format to provide trainings and support services in congregational, ministry, and nonprofit settings, with appropriate credit to Luther Seminary. Any other usage without the express written consent of Luther Seminary is prohibited.

Cover image by gubernat on Getty Images. Used with permission.

Faith+Lead
Luther Seminary
2481 Como Avenue
St. Paul, MN 55108

faithlead.luthersem.edu

All Scripture verses are New Revised Standard Version (NRSV) unless otherwise noted.

Table of Contents

3 INTRODUCTION

13 LISTEN

29 RECONNECT

39 DEFINE

59 REFRAME

73 CULTIVATE

91 NEXT STEPS

Introduction

Why Faithful Innovation? **4**

Congregational Process **10**

―――――

The Way Forward

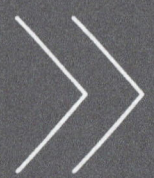
The way forward involves changing our thinking. The challenges facing congregations today are not ones that simply require technical fixes or a new program. Instead, they are adaptive challenges that demand new behaviors to help discover new ways of being the church. Rather than creating a new ministry or program, new learning is needed in order to adapt congregational life to connect more deeply with God, each other, and our neighbors. This is fundamentally theological and spiritual work.

Why Faithful Innovation?

The Current Landscape

Even before the pandemic, congregations around the United States were facing a number of challenges. These included challenges like struggling to form Christian community with members, children, and neighbors; a disconnect between church practice and people's daily lives; not knowing whether the congregation would exist for the next generation; or even thriving with lots of good things, but uncertainty about if they are "God things." A polarized political cycle damaged caring relationships through mistrust and a pandemic kept many of our congregations from meeting together for worship, weddings, and funerals.

All of these disruptive shifts impact congregational life. Many traditional ministry practices are breaking down, and traditional pastoral training does not translate well to the current leadership challenges. These realities require both opportunities for healing and innovation in the local church.

Connecting Faith to Everyday Life

While these shifts are new to many of our leaders, these types of challenges are not new to the church. God's law points out where things are breaking down and where we need healing. God's gospel promises that healing and new life will be a part of our future as God's people.

The people in our congregations and our communities are experiencing challenges in their lives and looking for ways to deal with these challenges.

When participation in the local church does not speak directly to those things that are "keeping them up at night," people look elsewhere for help and resources.

> The church must pursue faithful innovation as it seeks to connect God's presence and reality to the everyday lived experience of the people in congregations and communities.

Facing Adaptive Challenges

One thing that all of these challenges have in common is that they are adaptive in nature, rather than technical. Instead of simply requiring a new ministry or program, new learning is required in order to adapt congregational life to connect more deeply with God, each other, and our neighbors. This is fundamentally theological and spiritual work.

Learn More

What makes a challenge **adaptive**? What makes it **technical**? See page 46 for more information on the distinction between these two types of challenges.

Spiritual Practices and Tools

The following spiritual practices and tools are intended to foster deeper connections with God as the source of healing and hope in people's lives, both personally and communally. Rather than continuing to reflect the distraction, multi-tasking, and fatigue of contemporary life, practices of listening and reconnecting make it possible to clarify, focus, and simplify congregational life to engage the core spiritual and theological work.

We have collected these practices together in a process we call Leadership for Faithful Innovation that involves five key steps for leaders as they equip their people: **Listen**, **Reconnect**, **Define**, **Reframe**, and **Cultivate**. When ministry leaders take the time to refocus on the core spiritual and theological work through *listening* and *reconnecting*, the step of *defining* then leads to *reframing* unhelpful expectations placed upon pastors, as well as expectations of what it means to be a congregation member. A congregation is then able to *cultivate* an environment to try new behaviors of adapting and reshaping its life in order to participate more fully in God's mission in its context using a simplified process of **Listen-Act-Share**.

Throughout the faithful innovation process, congregations are empowered to discern where current practices are breaking down and where God's promises are bringing forth new possibilities and new life. Through these spiritual practices, members develop the capacity to join in God's work of creating and restoring Christian community in daily life.

Learn More

Go to pages 10-11 to learn more about Listen-Act-Share.

The Centrality of Discipleship

Following Jesus is not optional for today's church.

The Christian life is an invitation to embody a particular identity and way of being. Paul talks about this as being "in Christ." Through the power of the Holy Spirit, all believers receive the gift of God's grace and are joined into a community of transformation for the sake of the world.

For many inherited churches, congregational life has not necessarily been focused around offering a clear vision of Christian discipleship and the practices by which it is cultivated and expressed in daily life. The social contract for congregation members has concentrated more on supporting and sustaining the institution of the congregation, sometimes functioning primarily as a social and cultural organization.

For some people, the word "ministry" may be used restrictively to describe the work of an ordained leader or church staff person. In order for them to reframe their definition and role in the ministry of the congregation, they need to develop a theological understanding and vision of discipleship. At the same time, ordained leaders and staff may need to reframe their expectations and definitions as well.

The Leadership for Faithful Innovation process is an invitation to engage your leaders and members in a conversation to explore how your church understands and intends to live out the role of disciple.

Each Christian tradition has its own gifts and understandings of discipleship. We encourage you to identify those resources and make use of them in this work.

Learn More

Use the worksheet on pages 7-8 to examine your current congregational practices and consider whether they are contributing to the formation of Christian identity.

Workspace

Are You Ready?

Answer the following questions honestly to help you understand whether any current practices in your congregation are getting in the way of vitality and faithful innovation in your context.

When people are baptized or brought into your faith community, what promises do they make, and what promises are received?

What work of the church is available to members of a congregation? What work is reserved for ordained leadership?

When you read scripture that describes the future as God intends, what role do current Christians have in living into that reality?

What work of the church is currently done by ordained leaders or staff? What work is done by members? Why is this so? How does this fit (or not) with your scriptural, theological, traditional, and experiential understanding of discipleship?

How do congregational members learn about, and personally practice, the ways of following Jesus in their everyday lives?

How We Get There

Faithful innovation is the process of learning new ways to embody Christian identity and purpose in a changing cultural context. It often involves the rediscovery of ancient spiritual practices as much as the embrace of new technologies.

Rather than only relying on the faith and work of one leader, the way forward involves whole congregations cultivating life together through spiritual practices and innovation focused on discerning God's presence and joining God's work. Leaders encourage congregational members to engage in spiritual practices alongside practices of experimenting, prototyping, testing, and evaluating to cultivate faithful new expressions of ministry.

The three congregational practices of **Listen-Act-Share** help us discover how to make deeper connections to God, each other, and our neighbors. They help us discover what God might be up to in our context, promote personal spiritual growth, and allow us to experience a new way to be church.

> The hoped-for result of the faithful innovation process is to help congregations make deeper connections with God, each other, and their neighbors, and to have congregations experience being the church in a new way.

Congregational Process

Cultivating Christian Identity

What does this process look like in practice in our congregations and ministry settings?

We believe the Holy Spirit is moving ahead of the church, calling the church into a new future in a time of disruptive social and cultural change. This presents some new leadership challenges for the local church.

These leadership challenges cannot be addressed by one leader or staff; moving through these challenges requires participation by disciples who are cultivating the Christian identity of their community. A **Guiding Team** of 4-8 lay leaders guides their congregation to participate in a learning community process and the faithful innovation practices below.

A **Faithful Innovation Learning Community** is a peer-learning community of congregations who journey together. We employ ancient spiritual practices and cutting-edge innovation theory as we engage three key practices: *Listening, Action Learning, and Sharing Stories*.

These three practices of **Listen-Act-Share** help us discover how to make deeper connections to God, each other, and our neighbors. They help us discover what God might be up to in our context, promote personal spiritual growth, and allow us to experience a new way to be church.

While we find that it is helpful to encounter these practices in this order, **it is possible to start with *any* of these phases.**

For example, a congregation that is already experimenting because of a disruption may find it helpful to start by sharing what they are learning and experiencing, and then move into learning how to listen deeply.

Phases of Listening, Acting, and Sharing

LISTEN    ACT    SHARE

Listening—Tracing God's Movement in Our Lives and Neighborhoods

These practices equip participants to listen to God, their neighbors, and each other in their local contexts. Participants will dwell in Scripture together, share stories about what God is doing in the life of their local church, and notice where God might be at work in their everyday lives. The goal for these practices is to help the participants begin to answer the question "What might God be up to?"

Acting—Using Action Learning to Discover God's Leading

In this phase, the practices help participants use action learning to deepen their exploration of what they think God might be up to. The idea is to help participants "behave their way into new thinking" rather than only trying to think their way into new behaviors. Participants will be given simple action learning experiments to try in their neighborhood and are encouraged to invite congregation members to join in as well.

Sharing—Sharing Stories about What We've Learned

The practices in this phase help participants share what they've learned from the action learning experiments they did. A key practice that is too often left out of processes of congregational change is the simple but powerful step of reflecting on what was done and what was learned from it.

Without this practice of reflection getting into the bones and rhythms of a congregation's life, the first two practices of "listen" and "act" will be little more than a moment of trying something before moving on to something else. Sharing the stories of what was done and learned is where we see transformation beginning to unfold in congregations as we see what God might be teaching us!

What Comes Next?

After going through this process once, participants have several options. You can do the entire process again inviting the whole congregation to participate next time. Or you can choose an existing ministry within your congregation to intentionally do this process with.

When it comes to the Guiding Team, you can keep the same Guiding Team members or invite new ones to join the process. You can even have your current Guiding Team facilitate the trainings for others in your congregation.

The possibilities are truly endless when we are discerning what God is up to in our community and how we can partner with God as disciples of Jesus.

Listen

Dwelling in the Word **15**

Dwelling in the World **18**

Listening to Longings and Losses **20**

Listening to Spiritual Stories **23**

The Way Forward

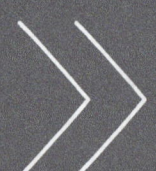

The way forward begins with listening: listening to God, listening to each other, listening to ourselves, and listening to the world around us. Listening to God together through Dwelling in the Word and Dwelling in the World helps us begin to name what God might already be up to in our midst. Listening to stories about what we long for and what we've lost (or are afraid to lose) as well as listening to the church community, neighbors, and community leaders help our hearts align with what God cares about most.

Workspace

Are You Ready?

Answer the following questions honestly to discern your level of engagement with the practices in this section. If you can answer the questions easily, you might be ready to move on to the next section. If not, this section might be a good place to focus right now.

Where might God be active in your congregation?

What might God be saying to you in and through the Scriptures right now?

How do your neighbors think God is active (if at all) in the neighborhood?

What recommendations do community leaders have for your local church regarding how to better connect with residents and constructively participate in community life right now?

Dwelling in the Word

When we seek to find out where God might be active in our local communities and in our daily lives, and as we consider where to join in with that work, one of the core practices to engage in is Dwelling in the Word. When we Dwell in the Word together, we listen to Scripture together, and we allow God to speak to us through it. Dwelling in the Word is an ancient way of reading the Scripture. It is a way of spiritually submitting to the text as one way God speaks to us, with a willingness to be shaped by what God might want to say through the Scripture. In this way, we are being interpreted by the text together as we listen to it.

All scripture is inspired by God and is useful for teaching, for reproof, for correction, and for training in righteousness, so that everyone who belongs to God may be proficient, equipped for every good work.
2 Timothy 3:16-17

Dwelling in the Word

An Ancient Practice

Dwelling in the Word is an ancient way of reading Scripture. It involves spiritually submitting to the text as one way God speaks to us, with a willingness to be shaped by what God might want to say through the Scripture. In this way, we are being interpreted by the text together as we listen to it.[1]

Three questions guide our listening:

1. What caught your attention?
2. What questions does this passage create for you?
3. What do you think God might be saying to you or to us through this passage?

The Dwelling Process

Listen to the Word together:

- Pray that God would speak to us
- Read the text, slowly
- Allow for silence
- Read again
- Allow for silence

Listen to someone else:

In-person version
- Find one person you can share your thoughts about the text with—a "reasonably friendly looking stranger," someone you maybe don't know well.
- Spend 4-5 minutes each sharing about what caught your imagination, or a question you have, or what you think the Spirit might be saying.

Online version
- In virtual breakout rooms, pair up with another person that you can share your thoughts about the text with.
- Spend 4-5 minutes each sharing about what caught your imagination, or a question you have, or what you think the Spirit might be saying.

Share in a group:

- In a group of 6-8 people, share what you heard your conversation partner say.
- Consider what God might be saying to you as a group—what are you hearing?

---

[1] This is a variation on a practice developed by Church Innovations Institute, www.churchinnovations.org/dwelling-in-the-word.

Choosing a Text

Selecting a text for Dwelling in the Word is often as important as the practice itself. You and your Guiding Team may choose to follow your denomination's liturgical calendar, like the ELCA Revised Common Lectionary, by drawing your material from the assigned weekly texts.

Or you may want to select texts that are thematically relevant to the issues or challenges your team is presently facing. The suggested texts below include themes of provision, comfort, trust, fruitfulness, growth, and hope. There are many options beyond these; this list represents verses that have been used repeatedly by the Faith+Lead team.

Suggested texts:

- Exodus 3:1-10 (Moses and the burning bush)
- Exodus 16:1-5,11-20,31 (manna and quail in the desert)
- 1 Kings 19:4-13 (God and Elijah in the wilderness)
- Isaiah 40:1-11 (comfort for God's people)
- Jeremiah 29:1,4-7 (exiled Israelites in Babylon)
- Matthew 13:24-30,36-43 (parable of the weeds)
- Mark 4:1-9 (parable of the sower)
- Luke 10:1-12 (mission of the seventy disciples)
- John 15:1-11 (Jesus as the true vine)
- Acts 8:26-40 (Philip and the Ethiopian eunuch)
- Acts 16:6-15 (Paul's journey to Macedonia)
- Romans 8:12-25 (heirs with Christ and future glory)

Dwelling in a Single Text

Many ministry leaders report having rich experiences by staying with a single text over a season, which could be several weeks to several months in length. By repeatedly exposing ourselves to the same passage, we open space for God to reveal how the text is transforming us over time. Words and phrases that once seemed familiar can take on new and deeper meaning as we discover the living power of God's Word.

Invite the Spirit's Leading

No matter how you choose to select your text or how long you read the same passage, invite the Spirit to lead you and your Guiding Team toward finding the text that God will use to speak to you. The entire purpose of the Dwelling practice is to enter into fellowship with God and to listen for God's voice. Be ready to discern the Spirit's movement through what you hear!

Dwelling in the World

When we are beginning to name what God might be up to in our midst, the simple practice of reflecting on everyday activities can help us begin to name God's presence and activity. Dwelling in the World is a simple practice of reflecting on God's movement in our daily lives in conversation with a partner.

Where can I go from your spirit? Or where can I flee from your presence? If I ascend to heaven, you are there; if I make my bed in Sheol, you are there. If I take the wings of the morning and settle at the farthest limits of the sea, even there your hand shall lead me, and your right hand shall hold me fast. If I say, "Surely the darkness shall cover me, and the light around me become night," even the darkness is not dark to you; the night is as bright as the day, for darkness is as light to you.

Psalm 139:7-12

Dwelling in the World

Dwelling in the World is a simple practice of reflecting on God's movement in our daily lives in conversation with a partner.

Step 1: Reflect (several minutes in silence)

Reflect back on the previous week. When was there a time when you had an opportunity to share God's peace with someone? This could be a friend, stranger, colleague, neighbor, or family member.

- Go back imaginatively into that encounter. What might God have been up to there?
- If you were to reconnect with that person, what might God want to do?

Step 2: Share and Listen

Find a partner (preferably a reasonably friendly looking stranger!) and spend several minutes sharing your story and reflections.

Step 3: Regather and Listen

Those who feel so led may share highlights of their stories/wonderings/reflections with the larger group. Or, with permission from your partner, you may share your partner's story highlights.

Listening to Longings and Losses

This spiritual practice of lament invites participants to enter into a process of lamenting the longings and losses that accompany any type of change that occurs as we faithfully innovate. Fears of loss can prevent congregations from pursuing faithful innovation altogether. Lamenting can create space for grieving losses as well as building trust in God's direction for the future.

Why, my soul, are you downcast? Why so disturbed within me? Put your hope in God, for I will yet praise him, my Savior and my God.
                                      Psalm 42:5 NIV

Listening to Longings and Losses

A Spiritual Practice of Lament

Many clergy and congregations long for their ministry to look differently than it currently does. Some want things to look like they "used to." Others want to see changes in how the congregation is led, who participates, or what the congregation focuses on.

Many clergy and congregations fear they are going to lose something important to them (or have lost something important) as the congregation faces the future. These fears are a reality for congregations who have questions about whether or not they will exist for another generation. These fears are also a reality in congregations that are stable or thriving and want to keep things going the way they are into the future.

This spiritual practice invites participants to enter into a process of lamenting these longings and losses. Lamenting can create space for grieving losses and building trust in God's direction for the future. This is framed according to the basic structure of a lament psalm. We invite you to work through it for yourself but also to consider using it with groups within your congregation.

Begin with These Questions

What's one wish you have for your congregation?

What's something that used to happen (or used to be true) in the congregation that you wish would return?

What's one thing you fear might be lost as your congregation moves into the future?

What's something that has changed that you feel is a loss in the life of the congregation?

Lamenting Longings and Losses

Address God
Direct your lament to God, framing the conversation about your longings and losses as a prayer.

Complaint
Name what you long for and wish was true about your congregation. Name your fears about what has been or could be lost as you move into the future.

Confession
Confess your need for God's grace and forgiveness in your life.

Ask God for Help
Name what you want God to do for you. Express your longings and losses as a request.

Affirm Trust in God
Affirm your trust in God and God's leadership over the future of your congregation.

Promise to Praise God
Praise God for who God is, what God has done, and what God will do.

Listening to Spiritual Stories

Listening to each other is an essential practice for learning to ask different questions. As we learn to listen to each other well, we also increase our capacity to hear what God might be saying to us. By creating space to listen to others, we want to especially focus on hearing people's stories of a time when they were most spiritually engaged and energized in their experience of their local church. And in listening to each other's stories, our capacity increases for listening to God and what God might be up to.

When he saw the crowds, he had compassion for them, because they were harassed and helpless, like sheep without a shepherd. Then he said to his disciples, "The harvest is plentiful, but the laborers are few; therefore ask the Lord of the harvest to send out laborers into his harvest."

Matthew 9:36-38

Listening to Spiritual Stories

Listening to the church community, neighbors, and community leaders

People in Your Congregation

Ask people in your congregation about when they have felt most spiritually alive. Write down some notes you can share with your team.

Here is a possible introduction to your conversation:

"I am interested in learning more about how people experience God in their everyday lives. So I'm asking some people in our congregation a few questions about their spiritual lives. Thanks for being willing to talk to me."

Suggested questions:

Reflect on a time when you would say you grew spiritually in a significant way. Describe what was happening in that period of your life.

What was it about this time of your life that you think caused you to grow spiritually?

Was there something during this time of your life that you think God was trying to teach you or show you?

Where do you experience God's presence most often now? (i.e. in worship, in nature, in conversation with friends/family, in prayer, in Bible study, at yoga, etc.)

People in Your Neighborhood

Find a few neighbors who are willing to be interviewed for 15-20 minutes. Here are some questions you might want to ask your neighbor.

How would you define your neighborhood?

How long have you lived/worked in this neighborhood?

What do you appreciate the most about the neighborhood?

What's one challenge you think the neighborhood is facing?

What's one hope you have for the neighborhood?

How do you think God is present in the neighborhood, if at all?

Leaders in Your Community

Purpose

"I am a member of a local church that is located in this area of the city, and we are trying to develop more awareness of what is happening and what the issues are in the set of neighborhoods we are seeking to serve."

Process

- Schedule an appointment to conduct the interview (will take around 30 minutes, 40 at most).
- Introduce yourself and the purpose of the interview—answer any questions the interviewee might have regarding what your church is doing.
- Take detailed enough notes during the interview so that they can be submitted for further analysis and reflection.
- Thank the person for taking time to visit with you.

Person being interviewed by category: (check box)

___ Police person
___ Fire person
___ Principal or school teacher
___ Business owner/leader
___ Political leader
___ Religious leader
___ Community organization leader
___ Other

Protocol

List the following:

Name of the person being interviewed

Their professional role/title

Name the organization they represent

Suggested Questions

Please tell me a little about your job. What are the primary responsibilities related to your work?

What most brings you satisfaction, both professionally and personally, in your job?

What are the two or three most significant challenges associated with you doing your job?

How would you assess the "quality of life" for community residents living in this area of the city? What are the primary trends and issues which are currently impacting this quality of life—whether for the good or for the bad?

What recommendations would you have for our local church regarding how to better connect with community residents and participate in constructive ways with community life?

What have we not discussed which would be helpful for me to know about in terms of our church working in this area of the city?

Reconnect

Chapters Exercise—Naming God's Presence and Activity Over Time **31**

Walking Your Neighborhood Exercise **33**

Trusting God and Taking a Risk **35**

The Way Forward

The way forward involves reconnecting with God's faithfulness, God's story, and God's promises to us as God's people. Moving into God's preferred future means connecting our current story with God's story. There is a distinctly Christian way to approach the future—by affirming God's leadership and God's abundance in our lives. The stories we tell ourselves must be shaped by God's stories and promises. We believe that God will show us the way forward and provide the resources needed to go there. We will continue to dwell in the world as God reconnects us with the neighborhood. This set of practices involves making explicit connections between the characters, events, and symbols of the biblical story and a congregation's story.

Workspace

Are You Ready?

Answer the following questions honestly to discern your level of engagement with the practices in this section. If you can answer the questions easily, you might be ready to move on to the next section. If not, this section might be a good place to target your focus right now.

In light of the history of your church and God's presence during that time, what do you think the next chapter in the life of your church looks like?

What might God be up to in your neighborhood?

What is one next step God is inviting you to take?

Who will help you take this next step?

RECONNECT »

Chapters Exercise— Naming God's Presence and Activity Over Time

The point of the "chapters exercise" is to use a narrative framework for reflecting back on the history of a particular congregation in order to name ways God might have been present and active over the course of its history. This helps build capacity for naming God's action in the midst of the congregation's life today.

Therefore, since we are surrounded by so great a cloud of witnesses, let us also lay aside every weight and the sin that clings so closely, and let us run with perseverance the race that is set before us, looking to Jesus the pioneer and perfecter of our faith, who for the sake of the joy that was set before him endured the cross, disregarding its shame, and has taken his seat at the right hand of the throne of God. Consider him who endured such hostility against himself from sinners, so that you may not grow weary or lose heart.
Hebrews 12:1–3

Chapters Exercise—Naming God's Presence and Activity Over Time

The point of the "chapters exercise" is to use a narrative framework for reflecting back on the history of a particular congregation in order to name ways God might have been present and active over the course of its history. This helps build up capacity for naming God's action in the midst of the congregation's current life.[1]

Exercise Steps

Introduction
Imagine that the history of this congregation is going to be made into a book. You are going to reflect on the history and create an outline of the life story of this congregation. Our outline will be made up of chapters that begin and end and have chapter titles. Do your best to remember as far back as you can.

Step 1: Determine what year the congregation began.

Step 2: Describe, to the best of your ability, what the early life of the church was like (i.e. who was there, why did they start, where did they meet, who were the key leaders, etc.).

Step 3: When do you think this "first chapter" of the church's life came to an end?

Step 4: What would you call the first chapter?

Step 5: What happened in the second chapter of the church's life?

Step 6: When did that chapter end?

Step 7: What would you call that chapter?

Repeat steps 5-7 until you reach the present day.

Now go back over your description of the life of this church. In each chapter, how do you think God was particularly active or present? What was God's role in each chapter? What might God have been up to during each chapter? Go through and write down a sentence or two about what you think God might have been up to during each chapter.

Final Step
In light of the history of this church and God's presence during that time, what do you think the next chapter in the life of this church looks like? What do you think God might be up to in the next chapter of the life of this church?

---

[1] This exercise was developed by Dr. Craig Van Gelder, Professor Emeritus of Congregational Mission at Luther Seminary.

RECONNECT »

Walking Your Neighborhood Exercise

In this practice, people are given tools to help them become more aware of the neighborhood where they live and/or the neighborhood around the church building. They will be given a map where they can fill in who lives and works around their church building and their home. They will be given instructions on how to walk or drive around their neighborhood and take pictures of things that represent something they think God might care about. They will make a list of gatherings that are led by people in the neighborhood that they could go and visit (i.e. like school events, government meetings, or neighborhood association gatherings). They will reflect on what they think God might be doing in these spaces.

And the Word became flesh and lived among us, and we have seen his glory, the glory as of a father's only son, full of grace and truth.
John 1:14

Walking Your Neighborhood Exercise

Listening to your neighborhood

Participate in a simple walk around your neighborhood. Study a map of the area and determine in advance the boundaries of where you will walk. Go with a group of 2-3 people and plan to walk for about 25 minutes.[1]

As you walk, consider the questions below to help you focus on listening. You may also wish to take a picture of something you think represents God's presence in the neighborhood. Share this image with your congregation.

Who is on the street?

What are people doing?

Are there things that surprise you?

What creates concern or questions?

Is there anything that catches your attention in a way that you want to ask more questions or get more information?

What do you think God might be doing in this neighborhood?

---

[1] This exercise was developed by Dr. Alan Roxburgh and The Missional Network, www.themissionalnetwork.com.

RECONNECT >>

Trusting God and Taking a Risk

The goal is to create space for intentional reflection on risk-taking as it relates to following God's lead. Doing something new always involves some measure of risk because we cannot know for certain what the outcome will be. Reconnecting with God's faithfulness reminds us that we can trust God and take a risk that God might be asking us to take in order to move forward.

"But the Advocate, the Holy Spirit, whom the Father will send in my name, will teach you everything, and remind you of all that I have said to you. Peace I leave with you; my peace I give to you. I do not give to you as the world gives. Do not let your hearts be troubled, and do not let them be afraid."

John 14:26-27

Trusting God and Taking a Risk

Naming where/how God might be asking you to trust in order to move forward

The goal of this exercise is to create space for intentional reflection on risk-taking as it relates to following God's lead.

What have you considered trying in your life but haven't had the courage or opportunity to do yet?

What is something that you've wanted to do in your life for many years but haven't ever pursued?

Is there anything you think God might be inviting you to try that you haven't stepped into yet?

List the reasons you haven't yet pursued these.

Name ways God has been faithful to you in the past.

What would need to be true of God in order for you to step out and take a risk on any of the things you wrote above?

If this were true about God, what is one step you could take towards something you think God might be inviting you to try that you haven't yet?

Define

What Keeps You Up at Night?	**41**
Empathy Map	**43**
Technical Problems and Adaptive Challenges	**45**
How Might We? (HMW)	**49**
Participation Analysis Tool	**55**

The Way Forward

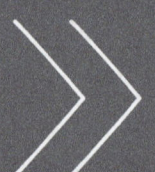

The way forward requires that we define the challenges we are facing in terms of God's agency in our lives. Many of the challenges we are facing are adaptive in nature—there are no easy answers because we don't yet know how to address them and because they require us to reflect on our assumptions and values. These are often the challenges that keep us up at night. Leaders need to articulate the challenges congregations are facing in ways that invite others to learn by doing in order to discern God's movement and God's call to a new way forward.

Workspace

Are You Ready?

Answer the following questions honestly to discern your level of engagement with the practices in this section. If you can answer the questions easily, you might be ready to move on to the next section. If not, this section might be a good place to target your focus right now.

What keeps you up at night?

What keeps your neighbors up at night?

What is your current adaptive challenge?

What are some "how might we" questions you have?

What one or two experiments are you trying in order to address this challenge?

What Keeps You Up at Night?

Ministry leaders face many different challenges, both in their work with their congregations and in balancing their personal lives. This exercise is designed to help you reflect on what is impacting you personally, as a leader, in your everyday life.

And after he had dismissed the crowds, he went up the mountain by himself to pray. When evening came, he was there alone, but by this time the boat, battered by the waves, was far from the land, for the wind was against them. And early in the morning he came walking toward them on the sea.
Matthew 14:23-25

What Keeps You Up at Night?

Ministry leaders face many different challenges, both in their work with their congregations and in balancing their personal lives. This exercise is designed to help you reflect on what is impacting you personally, as a leader, in your everyday life.

Take a minute and reflect on these two questions. Write down your answers and prepare to share some of your thoughts with a listening partner and others who support you. This will require some vulnerability!

What's one thing that "keeps you up at night?"

Why do you think this is something you're worried or concerned about?

DEFINE

Empathy Map

Defining the challenges congregations are facing requires more fully understanding what you and/or others are experiencing. This exercise is designed to help you see different facets of what people are experiencing in their daily lives.

When Jesus saw her weeping, and the Jews who had come along with her also weeping, he was deeply moved in spirit and troubled. "Where have you laid him?" he asked. "Come and see, Lord," they replied. Jesus wept.
John 11:33-35 NIV

Empathy Map

The following tool is intended to help you more fully understand what you and/or others are experiencing.

What are people in your congregation feeling?	What are people in your congregation spending the majority of their time doing?
What are people in your congregation yearning for?	What are some of the challenges people are facing?

What do people in your congregation need to focus on, in your opinion, in order for the church to move into a faithful future?

Technical Problems and Adaptive Challenges

Technical problems are those that can be addressed with existing resources and expertise. Adaptive challenges are those which have no easy answers but require new learning. They are challenges we must address together in order to move into the future. This exercise is designed to help you name a challenge you are facing in your church and then categorize it as primarily technical or primarily adaptive, based on your understanding of the challenge. This practice creates the space for thinking about creative, action learning-oriented ways to approach these adaptive challenges.

"I still have many things to say to you, but you cannot bear them now. When the Spirit of truth comes, he will guide you into all the truth; for he will not speak on his own, but will speak whatever he hears, and he will declare to you the things that are to come. He will glorify me, because he will take what is mine and declare it to you. All that the Father has is mine. For this reason I said that he will take what is mine and declare it to you."
John 16:12-15

Technical Problems and Adaptive Challenges

Technical problems are those that can be addressed with existing resources and expertise.

Adaptive challenges are those which have no easy answers but require new learning. They are challenges we must address together in order to move into the future.

Kind of challenge	Problem definition	Solution	Locus of work
Technical	Clear	Clear	Authority
Technical and adaptive	Clear	Requires learning	Authority and stakeholders
Adaptive	Requires learning	Requires learning	Stakeholders

Ronald Heifetz, Alexander Grashow and Marty Linsky, *The Practice of Adaptive Leadership*, p. 20.

Common Technical Problems
- "Our website needs updating."
- "We need to hire a new staff person."
- "Our building has some maintenance issues."
- "We need more volunteers in our kids' ministry."
- "We need to do a better job communicating the opportunities our church offers."

Examples of Adaptive Challenges
- "Our neighborhood has changed, and we don't know how to be in relationship with our new neighbors."
- "Established ways of worship and faith aren't speaking to younger generations and they are abandoning church. We don't know how to form Christian faith in their lives."
- "The congregational business model of membership, pledging, and volunteerism is breaking down, and we don't know what will replace it."
- "People in our congregation don't feel comfortable naming how they sense God's presence and activity in their daily lives."
- "Most of our congregations can't identify their source of hope."

Naming an Underlying Adaptive Challenge Worksheet

1. Describe the ministry challenge you are facing.

2. Ask the following questions of your ministry challenge.

Is the challenge we are facing clear, or does it require more learning?
- Clear challenge = more technical
- Unclear challenge = more adaptive

Does this challenge involve a problem that someone knows how to fix?
- Someone knows how to fix = more technical
- No known solution = more adaptive

Are we sure we understand the underlying cause of this challenge, or do we need to do more work to get to the root cause?
- Clear root cause = more technical
- Unclear root cause = more adaptive

Is there someone who has the authority to solve this challenge if they just decided to do so?
- Someone with authority can fix it = more technical
- No one has the authority to fix it = more adaptive

Or will this problem require the collaboration among those who are affected by the challenge?
- Doesn't require collaboration = more technical
- Requires collaboration = more adaptive

3. Restate the challenge in your own words.

4. Identify what is at stake and how we will likely need to change in order for the organization to be able to address this ministry challenge.

5. Now state what appears to be the *underlying* adaptive challenge which needs to be addressed but which we do not presently know how to address. Use the language "we don't know how to..."

DEFINE

How Might We? (HMW)

How Might We (HMW) is a method for framing questions once a challenge/problem statement has been identified. It is intended to help create space for a variety of approaches to a particular challenge to be articulated by a group. In the design process, we want to think expansively and avoid getting too focused on one solution too early.

When it grew late, his disciples came to him and said, "This is a deserted place, and the hour is now very late; send them away so that they may go into the surrounding country and villages and buy something for themselves to eat." But he answered them, "You give them something to eat." They said to him, "Are we to go and buy two hundred denarii worth of bread, and give it to them to eat?" And he said to them, "How many loaves have you? Go and see." When they had found out, they said, "Five, and two fish." Then he ordered them to get all the people to sit down in groups on the green grass.

Mark 6:35-39

How Might We? (HMW)

What is "How Might We (HMW)"?

HMW is a method in design thinking for framing questions once a challenge/problem statement has been identified. It is intended to help create space for a variety of approaches to a particular challenge to be articulated by a group. In the design thinking process, we want to think expansively and avoid getting too focused on one solution too early.

How? Might? We?

"How" suggests that we do not yet have the answer. "How" helps us set aside prescriptive briefs. "How" helps us explore a variety of endeavors instead of merely executing on what we "think" the solution should be.

"Might" emphasizes that our responses may only be possible solutions, not the only solution. "Might" also allows for exploration of multiple possible solutions, not settling for the first that comes to mind. We may well get some things wrong, and that is okay.

"We" immediately brings in the element of a collaborative effort. "We" suggests that the idea for the solution lies in our collective teamwork.[1]

---

[1] Content on this page is repurposed with permission from Interaction Design Foundation, www.interaction-design.org.

Creating "How How Might We" Questions

Creating a good HMW question requires thinking about the problem/challenge statement from a number of perspectives. The goal here is to create a lot of different possible HMW questions so that you can choose the one that you think fits the challenge the best.

Step 1: Write your challenge statement.

```
```

Step 2: Reflect on your challenge statement.

What are some of the root causes of this challenge?
-
-
-
-

What resources/assets do we have to utilize?
-
-
-
-

What are the emotions related to this challenge?
-
-
-
-

Step 3: Create How Might We (HMW) questions out of your challenge statement and the bullet points you created about your challenge above.

How might we..._____

How might we..._____

How might we..._____

How might we..._____

How might we..._____

How might we..._____

How might we..._____

How might we..._____

Tips for Creating Good HMW Questions

- Take the time to experiment with many different framings of the same problem. Much of the value of this exercise is in trying on new ways of framing.
- Strive for a balance between breadth and specificity of a "How Might We" question.
- Make sure your "How Might We" statement reflects some aspect of how you understand the problem. Providing context for a starting point will help you generate many more ideas than a general and broad statement of the challenge.
- Always use more than a single "How Might We"!

Creating "How Might We" Questions

Creating a good HMW question requires thinking about the problem/challenge statement from a number of perspectives. The goal here is to create a lot of different possible HMW questions so that you can choose the one that you think fits the challenge the best.

Step 1: Write your challenge statement.

> People in our congregations aren't comfortable talking about God.

Step 2: Reflect on your challenge statement.

> What are some of the root causes of this challenge?
> - People don't have lots of experience talking about God
> - People are afraid to offend others with "God language"
> - People don't want to say wrong things about God
> - People don't think about God that much outside of "church"

> What resources/assets do we have to utilize?
> - We can use language found in Scripture
> - Liturgy
> - Stories of people talking about God in a normal way

> What are the emotions related to this challenge?
> - Fear and anxiety
> - Uncertainty
> - Pressure to get it right

Step 3: Create How Might We (HMW) questions out of your challenge statement and the bullet points you created about your challenge above.

How might we... help people talk about God?

How might we... help people get more comfortable talking about God?

How might we... learn to talk about God ourselves?

How might we... listen to others talk about God?

How might we... create safe environments for people to talk about God?

How might we... help name the fears associated with "God talk"?

How might we... discuss with others why talking about God matters at all?

DEFINE

Participation Analysis Tool

Churches provide many activities for people in the congregation to participate in: worship services, Christian education classes, children's ministry events, small groups, service projects, etc. Each of these activities creates an environment that requires something from those participating. This is important to examine because faith formation is directly connected to whatever is essential for participation in the regular activities of the church. This tool helps leaders examine what is essential for participation in any given activity the church is engaged in.

Then Jesus said to the crowds and to his disciples, "The scribes and the Pharisees sit on Moses' seat; therefore, do whatever they teach you and follow it; but do not do as they do, for they do not practice what they teach. They tie up heavy burdens, hard to bear, and lay them on the shoulders of others; but they themselves are unwilling to lift a finger to move them."
Matthew 23:1-4

Participation Analysis Tool

What Does It Take to Participate?

Churches provide many activities for people in the congregation to participate in: worship services, Christian education classes, children's ministry events, small groups, service projects, etc. Each of these activities creates an environment that requires something from those participating. This tool helps leaders examine what is essential for participation in any given activity the church is engaged in.

This is important to examine because faith formation is directly connected to whatever is essential for participation in the regular activities of the church.

- **Activity Name:** What is this church activity called?
- **Activity Description:** What will someone do who is participating in this activity?
- **Activity Essentials:** What MUST someone know or do in order to participate in this activity?
- **Activity Formation:** If someone did this activity consistently over a year's time, what spiritual formation would they likely experience?
- **Activity Assessment:** If someone is doing this activity now, are they experiencing spiritual formation? How do you know? What are your feedback loops?

Example: Mid-Week Small Group Gathering

- **Activity Name:** Small Group Bible Study
- **Activity Description:** This group gathers together in the small group leader's home once per week. They meet for one hour. The group discusses one chapter from the book of Hebrews each week.
- **Activity Essentials:** Anyone participating in this activity must know the following things: how to get to the gathering place, some knowledge of the chapter being discussed, and the names/backgrounds of some of the people in the group.
- **Activity Formation:** Someone participating in this activity for a year would have a greater understanding of the book of Hebrews, deeper relationships with the people in the group, and a more significant connection to God through the Scripture.
- **Activity Assessment:** Solicit feedback from the participants to see how they are progressing. Convene an informal listening session to gauge what they're learning and the impact it's having on their spiritual formation.

Assignment

Identify one regular activity that people in your church participate in. Run your activity through these questions. Repeat this process with as many regular church activities as you have time for.

Participation Analysis Worksheet

Activity Name: What is this church activity called?

Activity Description: What will someone do who is participating in this activity?

Activity Essentials: What MUST someone know or do in order to participate in this activity?

Activity Formation: If someone did this activity consistently over a year's time, what spiritual formation would they likely experience?

Activity Assessment: If someone is doing this activity now, are they experiencing spiritual formation? How do you know? What are your feedback loops?

Reframe

Expectations Analysis Tool **61**

Design Thinking Process **64**

The Way Forward

The way forward requires that the church reframes expectations for both leaders and members. Change requires that we understand current expectations, negotiate new expectations, and empower leaders to focus their time and energy differently than they have in the past. Congregations must move beyond the clergy-centric performative model of ministry in order to engage in new ways of ministering. Empowering the laity is essential for engaging in faithful innovation. What do congregations currently expect their pastoral leaders to do? What does God expect from pastoral leaders and members if we are focused on faithful innovation and forming faith in the 21st century?

Workspace

Are You Ready?

Answer the following questions honestly to discern your level of engagement with the practices in this section. If you can answer the questions easily, you might be ready to move on to the next section. If not, this section might be a good place to target your focus right now.

In order for your congregation to take its next faithful step, what do you need to focus on?

What do congregants need to focus on?

Is there an "expectations gap" that needs to be addressed between what is essential and what the congregation expects of you (and of themselves) right now?

Expectations Analysis Tool

What do congregations expect of their pastoral leaders? What do pastoral leaders think congregations expect of them? How do pastoral leaders think these expectations need to change if they are going to be empowered to lead into the future? Is there an "expectations gap"?

So Christ himself gave the apostles, the prophets, the evangelists, the pastors and teachers, to equip his people for works of service, so that the body of Christ may be built up until we all reach unity in the faith and in the knowledge of the Son of God and become mature, attaining to the whole measure of the fullness of Christ.

Ephesians 4:11-13 NIV

Expectations Analysis Tool

Naming Current Expectations

What do you think congregations expect from their leaders and from themselves or each other as a community?

What do congregation members expect of you as a leader?	What do you expect of yourself as a leader?
What does the congregation expect of members?	What do you expect of congregation members?

Reflection and Reframing

1. Look back over what you have named above. Take some time to reflect on what you've listed about what others and you expect of you as a leader. Are these expectations fruitful and healthy? Are they what you need to focus on in order to help the congregation take its next faithful step?

Circle those you feel are most essential and life-giving (for the congregation and for you). Put **brackets** around those that you feel are unfruitful, unhealthy, or unnecessary.

2. Do the same thing with what you've named about expectations for congregation members. What's missing? Are these the things that congregation members should be focused on in order for the congregation to take its next faithful step?

Circle the things that you find most essential and life-giving. Put **brackets** around those that you feel are unfruitful, unhealthy, or unnecessary.

3. Make a **list** of the top 6-8 things that you think the congregation most needs you to focus on in order to help it take its next faithful step.

4. Make a **list** of the top 6-8 things that you think congregation members most need to focus on in order to take their next faithful step.

5. What are some things you might do as a leader to help reframe unhelpful expectations and refocus the congregation in the direction God is leading?

Design Thinking Process

You need more than strategic planning. This 5-step process helps you learn to design your actions through a process of listening and empathizing with the people in your congregation. Rather than starting with a predetermined outcome in mind, the design thinking process begins with listening, empathy, and lived experience as a way to understand what needs to happen next.

"Listen! A sower went out to sow. And as he sowed, some seed fell on the path, and the birds came and ate it up. Other seed fell on rocky ground, where it did not have much soil, and it sprang up quickly, since it had no depth of soil. And when the sun rose, it was scorched; and since it had no root, it withered away. Other seed fell among thorns, and the thorns grew up and choked it, and it yielded no grain. Other seed fell into good soil and brought forth grain, growing up and increasing and yielding thirty and sixty and a hundredfold." And he said, "Let anyone with ears to hear listen!"

Mark 4:3-9

Design Thinking Process

This 5-step process helps participants learn to design their actions through a process of listening and empathizing with the people their congregation engages. Rather than starting with a predetermined outcome in mind, the design thinking process begins with listening, empathy, and lived experience as a way to understand what needs to happen next.

Design thinking does not have a predetermined outcome or measure of success. For many, this process is uncomfortable, seems inefficient, and feels like wandering without direction. By some standards of learning it is, because much of our learning is in a controlled environment working towards a standard that is already determined.

For adaptive challenges, the standards are not yet known and the path is not clear. In such times, design thinking offers a disciplined process that keeps people at the center. It guides us without being prescriptive and requires a high level of adaptability. While learning and leading this way is not natural for most of us, it can be learned over time. Leaning into the process requires learning and reflecting on our own experience. Use the questions on the worksheet to process your experience.

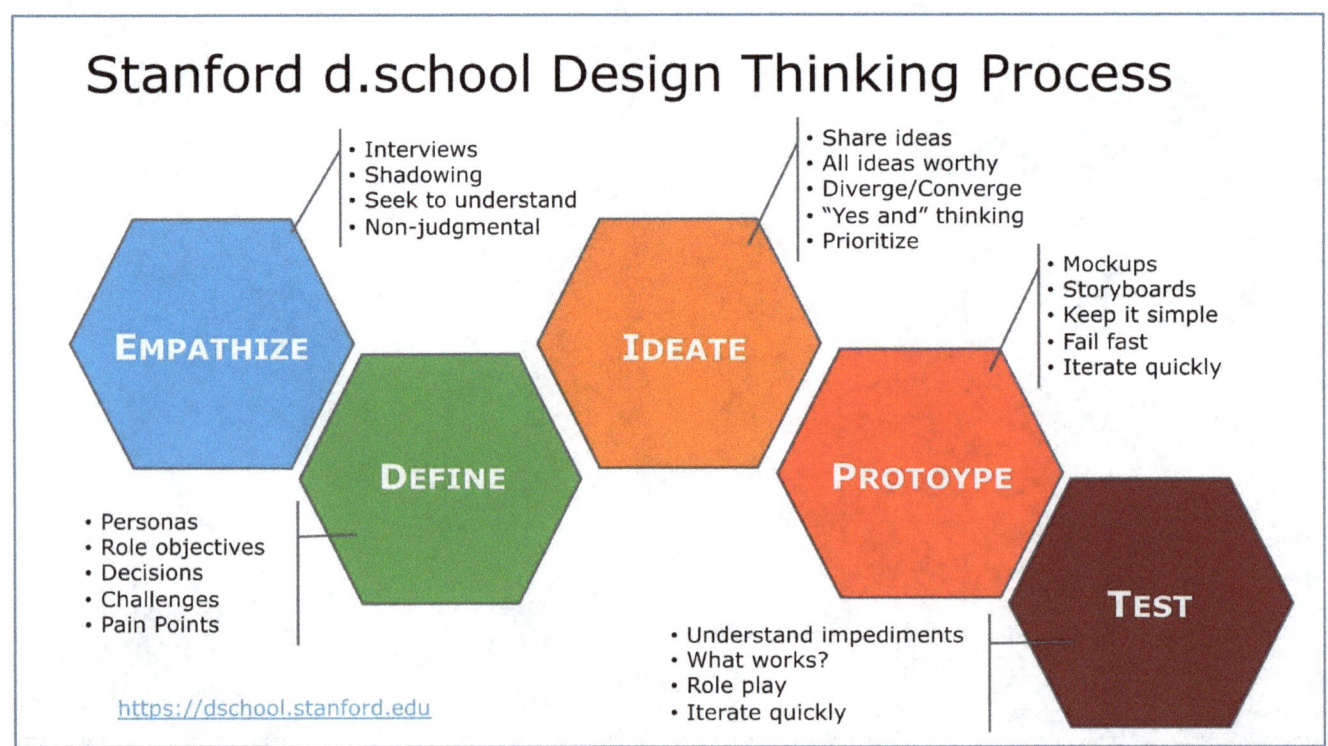

65

Empathize Exercise

Think of a complex ministry challenge in your context, one without easy answers or a simple solution. Write out the challenge below.

Human-centered design places people at the center of the design process, so think of a person (or persons) in your context to place at the center of your design process. Create a persona profile of this person (or a composite of several persons) using the prompts below.

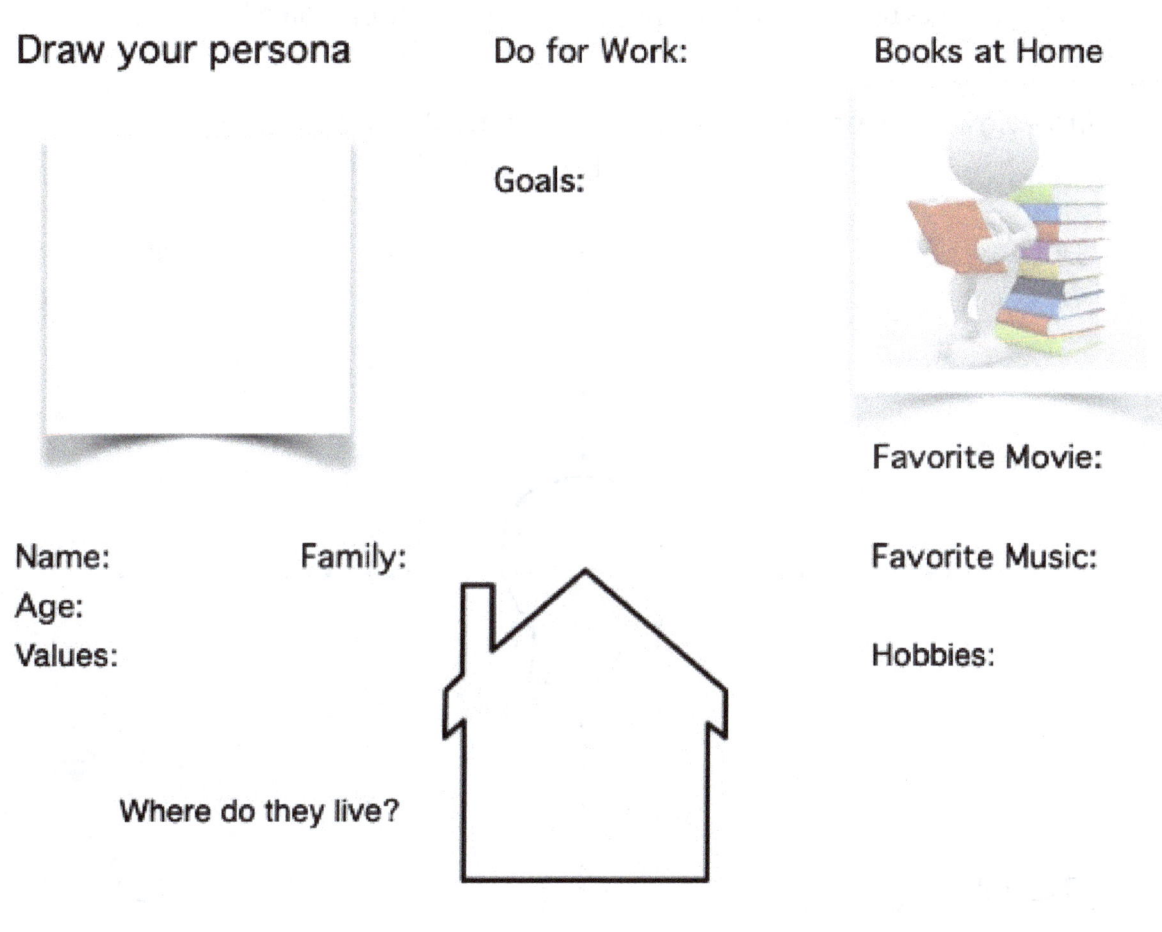

Make a list of 5-10 questions to help you better understand your persona related to your challenge.

Find a partner and have them take on your persona. Interview them using your list of questions. As you listen, hear what is said, notice what they do, probe deeply into their thinking, and delve into how they are feeling. Using the Empathy Mapping tool, make notes on what you learned about your persona. Then switch roles.[1]

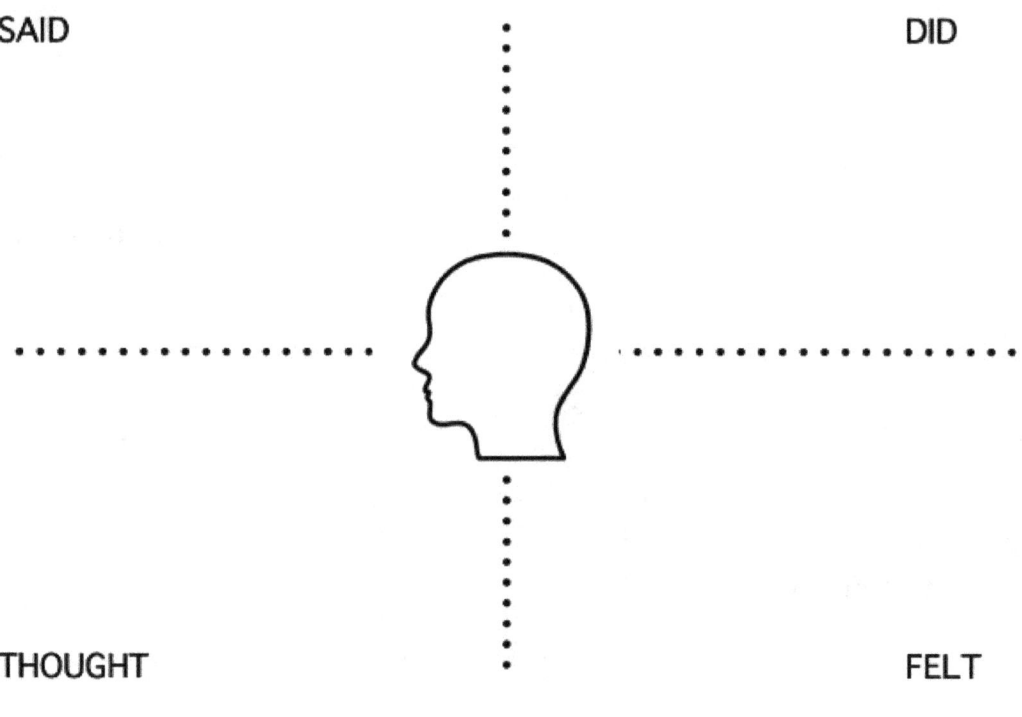

[1] Empathy mapping tool was adapted from Interaction Design Foundation, www.interaction-design.org/templates/empathy-map.

Define Exercise

This step of design thinking is crucial for honing the challenge. The Point of View (PoV) is a succinct statement regarding the problem to be solved. It weaves together the initial challenge with the learnings from the listening phase. It uses a MadLib format, naming the user, their needs, and your insights, to create a compass for the rest of the design process. While defining the problem is the second step of the process, it is common to adjust or revisit this step at various times throughout the process, either reinforcing the initial statement or adapting it as new information surfaces.

Point of View Statement

_____ needs to _____ because _____
(user)   (user's need)   (insight)

_____ needs to _____ because _____
(user)   (user's need)   (insight)

_____ needs to _____ because _____
(user)   (user's need)   (insight)

_____ needs to _____ because _____
(user)   (user's need)   (insight)

Ideate Exercise

The ideation stage starts with divergent thinking, or coming up with expansive and diverse ideas by brainstorming as many ideas as possible. The next step requires convergent thinking, or refining the ideas.

As the diagram below shows, we have already been through this pattern once. Brainstorming is often difficult without parameters, so this exercise will frame ideation around applying for a grant. To keep the challenge and persona front and center, rewrite both on the top of the worksheet. Then imagine addressing the challenge with a million dollar grant. In 5-7 minutes, come up with 10 ideas.

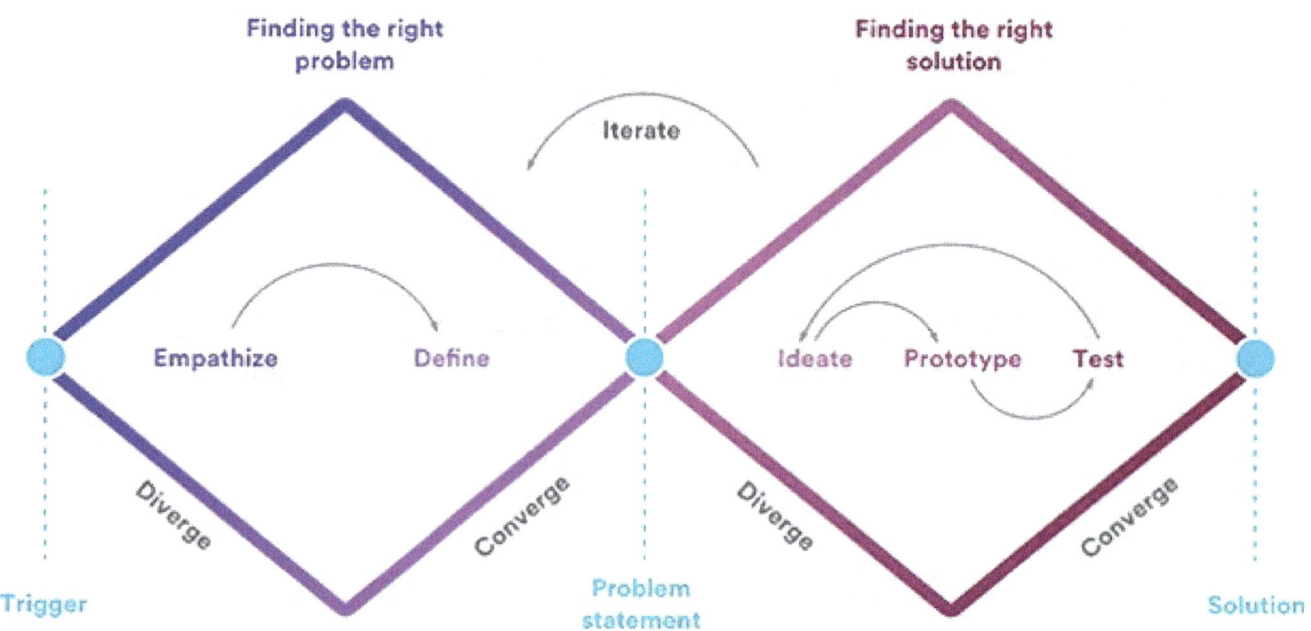

leanagileguru.com/category/design-thinking

- Give everyone a sheet of paper. Set a timer for 5-7 minutes. Have everyone come up with 10 solutions to your adaptive challenge.
- Have everyone leave their completed worksheet on the table so others can see it.
- Give everyone a strip of dots. Each dot counts for one vote.
- Have everyone stand up and go around the table reading each person's brainstorm ideas, placing stickers by the two ideas they like best.
- Set timer for 5 minutes, and don't overthink it—go with your gut reaction.

Ideate Example

You are applying for a $1 million grant to address:
Ministry with senior adults (adaptive challenge)

Rewrite your POV statement:
Senior adults need to serve because they need purpose.

Brainstorm ten way to address your challenge and POV:
1. Food truck ministry led by senior adults to share goods with the community.
2. Create a senior adult ministry collaborative with area churches. *
3. Create a team of senior adults available to care for children during worship.
4. Driving Ministry where senior adults take people who can't drive to appointments and other events. ****
5. Serve.com—create an online platform to post needs and people willing to serve.
6. Hire a ministry specialist to develop a service ministry. **
7. Match senior adults with young families in congregations to develop relationships and care for needs.
8. Curate projects senior adults can do at home, either online or to take home and return to the church.
9. Develop a senior adult band or theater company. ******
10. Create a senior adult university run and attended by seniors.

Prototype Exercise

Prototyping is learning with our hands. It moves ideas into concrete form. The sooner ideas get concrete, the sooner they are available for feedback. Take the ideas you generated in the Ideation Exercise along with the feedback received through the dot exercise and choose one idea to move forward. In 2-3 minutes sketch out three ideas for prototyping. Choose one to make into a prototype using the supplies on the table. Prototypes should be rough, and don't get too attached!

Test Exercise

Testing is about getting feedback in order to refine or redesign the prototypes. The more concrete and detailed the feedback the more helpful. Share your challenge/POV and prototype with 5-7 people in the congregation. Share a few details with them in the beginning in order to get their initial reactions. Let them engage the prototype. The three areas to gather specific feedback include: what they liked, what they wished for, and what they wondered about. Capture their feedback on a sheet of paper. Gather all the feedback and make any necessary adjustments.[1]

Feedback

I like...   I wish...   What if?

For this feedback, what did you learn?

Insights on your prototype

Insights on your user

Insights on your POV

---

[1] This exercise is based on material from Interaction Design Foundation, www.interaction-design.org/literature/article/test-your-prototypes-how-to-gather-feedback-and-maximise-learning.

Cultivate

Action Learning Experiments	**75**
Invitation to Risk-Taking	**78**
Discerning Prayer—Ignatian Examen	**81**
Spiritual Conversations	**84**
Neighborhood Engagement	**86**
Spiritual Exercises—Reflecting on God in Daily Life	**88**

The Way Forward

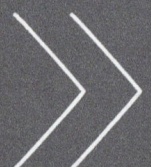

The way forward involves whole congregations cultivating life together through spiritual practices and innovation focused on discerning God's presence and joining God's work. Some of these spiritual practices are not new; they are actually ancient ways followers of Christ have experienced connection with God's Spirit. Alongside these are practices of experimenting, prototyping, testing, and evaluating that allow congregations to cultivate faithful new expressions of ministry.

Workspace

Are You Ready?

Answer the following questions honestly to discern your level of engagement with the practices in this section. If you can answer the questions easily, you might be ready to move on to the next section. If not, this section might be a good place to target your focus right now.

What spiritual practices are needed to help shape the life of your congregation right now?

What risks is God inviting your congregation to take?

What interdependent relationships do you have with your neighbors right now?

What does ongoing discipleship look like in your congregation such that people are listening to God's leading and acting upon it?

CULTIVATE »

Action Learning Experiments

An experiment in this process is a planned action-learning experience that is designed to help us "behave our way into new thinking." Experiments are the best way to learn when we are faced with challenges that require us to adapt and do something different than we have done it before. Experiments create space for us to discover new ways to be the church in our context. The outcome of the experiment—its success or failure—is far less important than what is learned through the action of conducting the experiment itself. Design your own experiments to address the adaptive challenges you have named in this process. Get members of your congregation involved in conducting the experiment with the goal of learning something new in the process.

After this the Lord appointed seventy others and sent them on ahead of him in pairs to every town and place where he himself intended to go. He said to them, "The harvest is plentiful, but the laborers are few; therefore ask the Lord of the harvest to send out laborers into his harvest."

Luke 10:1-2

Action Learning Experiments

What is an experiment?
An experiment in this process is a planned action-learning experience that is designed to help us "behave our way into new thinking."

What is the point of experiments?
Experiments are the best way to learn when we are faced with challenges that require us to adapt and do something differently than we have done it before. Experiments create space for us to discover new ways to be the church in our context.

What makes an experiment successful?
The success of an experiment is determined by how much we learn and are transformed by the experience rather than by how much impact our actions have on others.

How do you know what you've learned or how you've been transformed?
Once the experiment is finished, we create a feedback loop opportunity where we as participants gather to reflect on and share what we experienced or learned about God, ourselves, and others through the experiment. This intentional time of reflection will help us process what we've learned, how we've changed, and what we would like to share with others.

How do you design a good experiment?
There are 3 major steps to designing an experiment:
1. Name what you want to learn.
2. Describe the steps you will take in the experiment.
3. Create a feedback loop.

Experiment Design Worksheet

1. Name what you want to learn (learning objective). How is this based on your listening work?

2. Describe the steps you will take in the experiment.

3. Create a feedback loop.

Invitation to Risk-Taking

This practice invites you and your congregation to go beyond what you have done in this process and name some significant risk you believe God may be inviting you to take in the next season/chapter of the life of the congregation.

But when the disciples saw him walking on the sea, they were terrified, saying, "It is a ghost!" And they cried out in fear. But immediately Jesus spoke to them and said, "Take heart, it is I; do not be afraid." Peter answered him, "Lord, if it is you, command me to come to you on the water." He said, "Come." So Peter got out of the boat, started walking on the water, and came toward Jesus. But when he noticed the strong wind, he became frightened, and beginning to sink, he cried out, "Lord, save me!" Jesus immediately reached out his hand and caught him, saying to him, "You of little faith, why did you doubt?"

Matthew 14:26-31

Invitation to Risk-Taking

Naming where/how God might be asking your congregation to trust in order to move forward

The goal is for your congregation to go beyond what you have done in this process and name some significant risk you believe God may be inviting you to take in the next season/chapter in the life of the congregation.

What might God be inviting your congregation to do but you haven't had the courage or opportunity to do yet?

What is something that the congregation has been wanting to do for a long time but hasn't ever pursued?

Is there anything you think God might be inviting the congregation to try that you haven't stepped out and tried yet?

List the reasons you haven't yet pursued these.

Name ways God has led the congregation in the past.

What is one step the congregation could take towards something you think God might be inviting the congregation to try that it hasn't yet?

CULTIVATE >>

Discerning Prayer—Ignatian Examen

This practice creates space for groups of participants to listen and discuss together what God might be leading them to do as a group and as individuals.

I remember the days of old, I think about all your deeds, I meditate on the works of your hands.

Psalm 143:5

Discerning Prayer—Ignatian Examen

Simplified Practice

The Ignatian Examen is a centuries-old way of reflecting back on your experience of the previous day (or previous week) and tracing God's movement in your life.

1. Become aware of God's presence. How are you experiencing God's presence with you in this moment?

2. Reflect back on the previous day (or week). What were the most life-giving moments? What brought you closer to God and others?

3. As you continue to reflect, what were the most life-taking moments? What drew you apart from God and others?

4. Lift up to God in prayer what you've just named. You may wish to write out your prayer below.

5. As you think about the rest of this day and the day to come, what's one step you can take to be more aware of and trust in God's presence?

CULTIVATE

Spiritual Conversations

This practice helps participants gain more confidence and comfort in talking about God in normal conversations. You are encouraged to name how people see God at work in their everyday lives in ways that would make sense to those who don't share their faith background.

Now when Jesus came into the district of Caesarea Philippi, he asked his disciples, "Who do people say that the Son of Man is?" And they said, "Some say John the Baptist, but others Elijah, and still others Jeremiah or one of the prophets." He said to them, "But who do you say that I am?" Simon Peter answered, "You are the Messiah, the Son of the living God."
Matthew 16:13-16

Spiritual Conversations

Why Jesus? A Spiritual Practice for Telling and Hearing Stories of Faith

GATHER A GROUP OF FRIENDS
This can be an adult forum or small group, or even something totally informal. Plan at least a few gatherings. Bonus: serve food!

BEGIN WITH PRAYER
Ask someone to start off right by thanking God for those gathered and praying for the Holy Spirit's presence.

EACH TIME YOU GATHER, ASK ONE PERSON TO SPEAK
Have them prepare a 15-20 minute testimony answering two questions: Why am I a Christian? What difference does Jesus make in my life?

GET INTO GROUPS OF 2-3 AND REFLECT TOGETHER
Choose one question and go deep for about 15 minutes: What caught your imagination in the story you heard? Where did you see God at work in the storyteller's life? What difference did Jesus make in your life this week?

COME BACK TOGETHER AND SHARE
Convene the entire group again for ten minutes to talk about the experience. Answer the question, What was this like to do?

Neighborhood Engagement

This practice asks questions about the ongoing relational engagement of your congregation with "the neighborhood." It assumes that every congregation is called to "love its neighbor as itself" and creates space for naming how that will be pursued. This goes beyond providing resources to the community and invites your congregation to consider what a reciprocal interdependent relationship with the neighborhood could be like.

Jesus replied: "'Love the Lord your God with all your heart and with all your soul and with all your mind.' This is the first and greatest commandment. And the second is like it: 'Love your neighbor as yourself.' All the Law and the Prophets hang on these two commandments."
                                    Matthew 22:37-40 NIV

Neighborhood Engagement

What is neighborhood engagement?

In this process, our assumption is that every Christian community is called to love their neighbor as they love themselves. Doing so means having a relationship with the neighborhood that is mutually beneficial.

What makes neighborhood engagement successful?

The success of neighborhood engagement is determined by how we partner with what God is already up to and by having interdependent relationships with the neighborhood.

1. Name how you think God might be calling your congregation to engage in the neighborhood. How is this based on your listening work?

2. Describe how this is loving your neighbors.

3. Create a feedback loop to ensure this is based on an interdependent relationship with your neighbors.

Spiritual Exercises—Reflecting on God in Daily Life

Choose from some of the spiritual practices introduced throughout this guide to incorporate into the life of your congregation (i.e. Dwelling in the Word, Ignatian Examen, Dwelling in the World, etc.). The goal is to name which spiritual practices can help shape the ongoing life of your congregation.

And I pray that you, being rooted and established in love, may have power, together with all the Lord's holy people, to grasp how wide and long and high and deep is the love of Christ, and to know this love that surpasses knowledge—that you may be filled to the measure of all the fullness of God.
Ephesians 3:17b-19 NIV

Spiritual Exercises—Reflecting on God in Daily Life

Choose from some of the spiritual practices introduced throughout this guide to incorporate into the life of your congregation (i.e. Dwelling in the World, Ignatian Examen, Dwelling in the Word, etc.).

Which practice did you choose? Why?

How might you incorporate this practice into the daily life of your congregation?

How can this practice help shape the ongoing life of your congregation?

Next Steps

Prayer and Personal Reflection **92**

Discipleship in Your Congregation **94**

For More Information **96**

The Way Forward

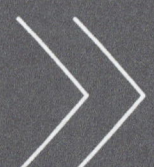 The way forward in the Faithful Innovation process is to keep going as the spiritual practices become a way of life for you and your congregation. The point isn't to "arrive" at a destination but to be transformed into Christ-likeness as you draw near to God over time. This is important work—arguably the most important you and the people you serve will ever do. Go forth in confidence that God is with you and continue to seek God's guidance and presence. God is beside you and for you.

NEXT STEPS >>

Prayer and Personal Reflection

Your own formation is a crucial part of this process. This practice invites you to consider how God has impacted your life, where you are in your journey, the kinds of questions you're asking in this moment, and how what you've learned (and are learning) has affected your leadership.

So if anyone is in Christ, there is a new creation: everything old has passed away; see, everything has become new!
                                           2 Corinthians 5:17

Prayer and Personal Reflection

Take a few moments to reflect on your own faith formation.

What's one way God has impacted your life?

What questions are you asking right now? Are they theological, personal, relational, social, or strategic questions?

Where in your life and ministry does it seem like the seed is falling on good soil?

Are there ways God is inviting you to lead differently in light of what you are learning? What are they?

NEXT STEPS

Discipleship in Your Congregation

Choose from some of the practices introduced throughout this guide to incorporate into the life of your congregation. The goal is to name how you will continuously equip and empower people in the life and ministry of your congregation to listen to God's leading and have the courage to act on that leading together. What does ongoing discipleship look like in the life of this congregation?

And Jesus came and said to them, "All authority in heaven and on earth has been given to me. Go therefore and make disciples of all nations, baptizing them in the name of the Father and of the Son and of the Holy Spirit, and teaching them to obey everything that I have commanded you. And remember, I am with you always, to the end of the age."
                                    Matthew 28:18-20

Discipleship in Your Congregation

Choose from some of the practices introduced throughout this guide to incorporate into the life of your congregation.

Which practice did you choose? Why?

How might you continuously equip and empower people engaged in the life and ministry of your congregation to listen to God's leading and have the courage to act on that leading together?

How might the practice you have chosen help you do this?

What does ongoing discipleship look like in the life of your congregation?

For More Information

Faith+Lead Team

Want to learn more? Have questions?
Reach out to the Faith+Lead team for help.

Rev. Dr. Dawn Alitz
Director of Coaching and Events
dalitz002@luthersem.edu

Dr. Alicia Granholm
Director of Communities and Consulting
agranholm001@luthersem.edu

Tessa Pinkstaff
Project Manager
tpinkstaff001@luthersem.edu

Faith+Lead Website

Visit the Faith+Lead website for additional resources and information about Learning Communities offered through Luther Seminary.

faithlead.luthersem.edu

Faith+Lead Learning Laboratory

Join the interactive Faith+Lead Learning Laboratory to access courses, online communities, and other resources.

faithlead.mn.co

Where can you turn for help?

faith+lead
LUTHER SEMINARY

In a changing church and world, no one has all the answers. But together, we can discover the future into which God is calling us.

Get connected to an entire community of supportive Christian leaders on Faith+Lead, Luther Seminary's interactive learning hub.

Continue your journey.

faithlead.luthersem.edu

- Podcasts
- Videos
- Learning communities
- Courses
- Webinars
- Resources
- Spiritual practices
- Articles
- Blog posts
- Networking with faith leaders

Clergy coaching now available through Faith+Lead

faith+lead
LUTHER SEMINARY

A coach is a conversation partner who can hold sacred space, listen well, and reflect back to you your own wisdom.

Experience the life-changing gift of coaching and discover a path toward deepened self-knowledge, awareness of God's movement in your personal and vocational life, and next steps toward living into God's dream for you.

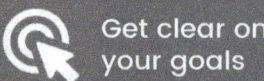 Get clear on your goals

 Find support and wisdom

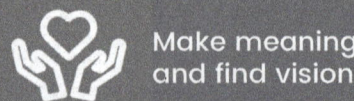 Make meaning and find vision

To learn more, request information, or set up a consultation, visit:

faithlead.luthersem.edu/coaching

CPSIA information can be obtained
at www.ICGtesting.com
Printed in the USA
LVHW060533220323
742182LV00009B/194